FUNNY HA-HA, FUNNY PECULIAR

Hilarious jokes to make you chortle out loud and bizarre facts to make you gasp in horror, wonder and amazement, covering every topic under the sun!

Printed and bound in Great Britain for Hodder and Stoughton Children's Books, a division of Hodder and Stoughton Ltd, Mill Road, Dunton Green, Sevenoaks, Kent TN13 2YA. (Editorial Office: 47 Bedford Square, London WC1B 3DP) by Cox and Wyman Ltd, Reading, Berks. Photoset by Rowland Phototypesetting Ltd, Bury St Edmunds, Suffolk.

British Library C.I.P.
Cataloguing in Publication Data is available from the British Library

ISBN 0 340 54161 X

FUNNY HA-HA
FUNNY PECULIAR

by
Ed Teacher
Illustrated by Alan Rowe

Knight Books
Hodder and Stoughton

What did Lot do when his wife was turned into a block of salt?
He put her in the cellar.

Who entertained Herod with the dance of the seven sausage skins?
Salami.

TEACHER: Who can tell me something of importance that did not exist at the time of Adam and Eve?
PUPIL: Me.

TEACHER: Who was the greatest entertainer in biblical times?
PUPIL: Samson. He brought the house down.

Josef Stalin, the Soviet ruler who abolished religion in the USSR, once trained for five years to be a priest.

In 1542 the costume-designer for the Coventry mystery play charged one shilling for making God's wig and tunic.

Psalm 117, verse 2 is the exact middle of the Bible, in terms of the number of words.

Miss Piggy, star of the *Muppet Show*, was banned from Turkish television during religious festivals so that viewers were spared the sight of an 'unclean' animal.

During the fifteenth century, men and women had to sit on either side of the aisle in church.

In the eleventh century, a Benedictine monk called Oliver of Malmesbury fitted himself with a pair of wings and jumped from the top of a high tower. He died.

The poet Byron learnt Cockney rhyming slang from an Italian cardinal who had never left Italy in his life.

According to ancient Muslim tradition, it wasn't an apple that Eve ate in the Garden of Eden, but a fig. In fact, there is no reference to an apple in the Bible.

Touching wood for good luck is a Christian practice. The wood symbolises the original cross on which Jesus died.

SPORTS MASTER: Why don't you try the high jump?
PUPIL: I'm scared of heights.

PUPIL: You played a great game.
TEAM MATE: I thought I played rather badly.
PUPIL: I meant you played a great game for the other side.

TEACHER: Who was the first woman on earth?
PUPIL: I don't know, sir.
TEACHER: Come on, it's got something to do with an apple.
PUPIL: Er, Granny Smith?

TEACHER: Who can tell me what BC stands for?
PUPIL: Before Calculators!

A survey of over 3,000 athletes showed that twenty-two per cent of them wear glasses.

Table tennis was originally played with a cork ball.

The first floodlit football league game was played in 1956.

Billiards was first played in Italy in 1550.

Arsenal Football Club was originally called Dial Square FC when it was set up in 1884.

Golf balls used to be stuffed with feathers. It took a top-hat full of them to stuff a single ball.

PUPIL: If there's a referee in football and an umpire in cricket, what do you have in bowls?
SPORTS MASTER: I have no idea.
PUPIL: Goldfish of course!

SPORTS MASTER: Why didn't you stop that ball?
PUPIL GOALKEEPER: I thought the net would stop it.

PUPIL: My new football boots hurt me.
SPORTS MASTER: I'm not surprised – you're wearing them on the wrong feet.
PUPIL: What can I do about that? These are the only feet I've got.

SPORTS MASTER: Who was the fastest runner in history?

PUPIL: Adam – he was the first in the human race.

Cricket was outlawed in 1477 by Edward IV.

Norwegian cross-country runner Mensen Ernst ran from Paris to Moscow in a fortnight. Swimming thirteen wide rivers, he still managed to average 200 kilometres a day.

Ostrich races are held in South Africa with jockeys mounted on saddles on the birds' backs.

Table tennis was first named 'gossamer'.

The game of chess originated in India.

Adelaide in Australia is named after King William IV's wife.

Who sat on crates in a train and wrote music?
Luggage Van Beethoven.

Why did the composer spend all his money?
He was on a Chopin spree.

How did the concert pianist feel when he lost his music?
Liszt-less.

Who painted the *Mona Lisa* and invented fizzy drinks?
Lemonade da Vinci.

What do you know about the great composers of the eighteenth century?
They are all dead.

The Queen is entertained by bagpipe music at breakfast each morning. A piper marches outside the dining-room window for ten minutes.

In 1831 the Italian operatic tenor Giovanni Rubini sang one high note with such force that he dislocated his collarbone.

A grand piano weighing one and a quarter tonnes was made in London in 1935.

The composer Schoenberg was born on 13 September, 1874, and believed that he would die on the thirteenth. He was also convinced that as the number six and seven add up to 13, he would die at the age of seventy-six. He died in 1951 – at 13 minutes before midnight on Friday 13 July, aged 76.

The composer Rossini was too nervous to travel by train.

Irving Berlin, America's most prolific songwriter, never learned to read or write music.

Ravel composed just 19 hours of music in 42 years.

Elgar used to go out driving with his three pet dogs on the back seat of his open-top car. All of them used to wear goggles.

The opera *Aida* was specially commissioned to celebrate the opening of the Suez Canal.

What's smelly and hums?
Beethoven's remains decomposing.

What's white and sweet and comes from outer space?
A Martian mallow.

What turned the moon pale?
Atmos-fear.

How do you phone the sun?
Use a sundial.

Which is the noisiest planet?
Saturn, because it has so many rings.

What's the death-rate on the moon?
Same as anywhere else – one death per person.

A French composer called Lully died after piercing his foot with the baton he used for conducting the orchestra and contracting blood poisoning.

The nearest galaxy to our own is Andromeda.

No one has ever seen a black hole.

The moon is older than the earth: the oldest moon rock dates back 5.3 billion years, compared with earth's 3.7 billion years.

The American writer Mark Twain was born when Halley's Comet appeared in 1835 – and died when it appeared again in 1910.

Red and blue moons make an appearance quite often due to dust in the atmosphere, but a green moon has only ever been seen once.

Antarctica is the coldest place on earth, but it still has an average temperature that is warmer than the daytime temperature on Mars.

Shooting stars are not stars at all, but meteors burning as they descend through the earth's atmosphere.

Jupiter has a day that lasts only nine hours and 50 minutes.

The planet Uranus can only just be seen by the naked eye.

What's big, bright and silly?
A fool moon.

What's brown and woolly and goes around the sun?
A Mars baaa!

Where's Yarmouth?
Same as yours – under my nose.

Who is blonde, sings and lives in South America?
Bolivia Newton-John.

What phantom was a famous painter?
Vincent Van Ghost.

Where do ghosts go for their holidays?
Goole.

Where do Egyptian mummies go for their holidays?
The Dead Sea.

Where do ghosts swim in North America?
Lake Eerie.

NERVOUS AIR PASSENGER: How often do planes of
this type crash?
AIR HOSTESS: Only once, madam.

Where are the Andes?
At the end of the wristies.

Because of the time that it takes for light to reach the earth, the sun rises eight minutes before we actually see it.

The earth spins faster on its axis in September than it does in March.

About 450 million years ago, the South Pole was situated not in Antarctica, but where the Sahara Desert is now.

Four of the shortest place-names in the world are Y (in France), A (in Sweden), U (in the Caroline Islands) and O (in Japan).

Spinach originated in Persia.

The whole of the American continent would fit into Asia with plenty of room to spare.

TEACHER: Why did primitive man draw pictures of animals on the walls of their caves?
PUPIL: Because they didn't know how to spell their names.

What's the cheapest way to get to China?
Be born there.

TEACHER: When was Rome built?
PUPIL: At night.
TEACHER: Why do you say that?
PUPIL: Because I read that Rome wasn't built in a day.

Who ruled Gaul and kept catching colds?
Julius Sneezer.

What was the most remarkable achievement of the Romans?
Learning Latin.

There are more lakes in Canada than in the rest of the world put together.

The two largest cities in the Netherlands – Amsterdam and Rotterdam – and half the area of the country lie below sea-level.

The Icelandic parliament, the Althing, was established in AD930 and has been governing the country for over a thousand years since.

More than a third of the world's commercial supply of pineapples are grown in Hawaii.

What did they call Julius Caesar on a foggy night in Scotland?
A Roman in the gloamin'.

How was the Roman Empire cut in half?
With a pair of Caesars.

What happened to Boudicca when she lost the battle?
Julius seized 'er.

Why did the Romans build straight roads?
So the Britons couldn't hide round the corners.

'Doctor, Doctor, I have a terrible allergy. Can you help me out?'
'Certainly – which way did you come in?'

'Doctor, Doctor, I keep hearing ringing in my ears.'
'Nonsense, you're as sound as a bell.'

'Doctor, Doctor, I keep seeing purple and pink spots.'
'Have you seen a psychiatrist?'
'No, only purple and pink spots.'

'Doctor, Doctor, I think I'm allergic to perfume.'
'Never mind, I'll have you scent to a psychiatrist.'

What's red, spreads and shouldn't be broken?
A rash promise.

What's good for nervous elephants?
Trunkquillizers.

The Roman emperor Nero is the only competitor in the history of the Olympics to have been awarded first place without winning his competition, or even completing the course.

Pontius Pilate is looked upon as a saint in the Ethiopian Church.

In cold climates, Roman soldiers used to sting themselves with nettles to make themselves feel warmer.

There were 144 public toilets in Rome in AD315.

Sausages were banned in Rome during the reign of the Christian emperor Constantine the Great because he thought they were pagan.

The Romans had a god for everything – including one who was supposed to protect crops from mildew.

The emperor Julius Caesar was so embarrassed by his baldness that he always wore a laurel wreath to disguise it.

The ancient Romans used lead in their food to make it easier to digest. They also used lead to cure stomach upsets!

Claudius, Emperor of Rome, died in the year AD54 after choking on a feather . . .

'Doctor, Doctor, I'm having trouble with my breathing.'
'I'll soon put a stop to that.'

'Doctor, Doctor, I think I'm allergic to liquorice.'
'Well, it takes Allsorts to make a world.'

'Doctor, Doctor, when I get up in the morning I'm always dizzy for half an hour.'
'Try getting up half an hour later.'

'Doctor, Doctor, I can't stop trembling.'
'I'll be with you in a couple of shakes.'

What do you give to someone who has everything?
Penicillin.

Don't throw away indigestion tablets – save them for a Rennie day.

Why do they make tablets round?
To avoid side effects.

'I started with pneumonia, then it was tonsillitis and appendicitis, and then they gave me penicillin and tranquillizers.'
'It sounds awful.'
'Yes, it was the worst spelling test I've ever had.'

'Why are you jumping up and down?'
'I took my medicine and forgot to shake the bottle.'

Nero hoped to improve his singing voice by eating leeks.

The designs adopted in medieval heraldry were based on symbols that Roman soldiers drew on their shields to ward off the evil eye.

By the age of 15, more than 95 per cent of teenagers have some form of permanent tooth decay. About 50 per cent of British people have lost their natural teeth by the time they are middle-aged . . .

The most common disease in the world is tooth decay. Each year British dentists extract about four tonnes of children's rotten teeth . . .

'Doctor, Doctor, can you give me something for wind?'
'Certainly – here's a kite.'

What is the best thing to take when you're run down?
The number of the car.

Doctors have just discovered a medicine that is so strong,
you have to be in perfect health to take it.

'Doctor, Doctor, can I have some more of those sleeping
pills for my wife? She's just woken up again.'

Medical studies have shown that more people catch colds by holding or shaking hands than by kissing.

Another study showed that people are more likely to catch colds when their mothers-in-law comes to stay.

Sneezes can sometimes travel at a hundred miles per hour.

The medical term for the common cold is 'nasopharyngitis'.

The common cold is estimated to cost the world's economy more than 10,000 million pounds a year in lost work time.

In 1979, 12-year-old Patricia Raey of Liverpool caught a cold and continued sneezing for a further 194 days before stopping.

Allan Pinkerton, founder of the famous Pinkerton detective agency, died in 1884 after stumbling during a walk, biting his tongue, and contracting gangrene . . .

Miss Phyllis Newcombe, a 22-year-old British girl, spontaneously burst into flames while waltzing in a dance hall in 1938 . . .

Zeuxis, a Greek painter from the fifth century BC, laughed so hard at his own painting of an ugly woman that he burst a blood vessel and died . . .

What's the difference between an elephant and an aspirin?
An aspirin is small and white.

What are wedge-shaped aspirins for?
For splitting headaches.

'Doctor, Doctor, what can you give me for my liver?'
'How about half a kilo of onions?'

'Doctor, Doctor, my husband thinks he's Moses.'
'Tell him to stop taking the Tablets.'

Why aren't there any aspirins in the jungle?
Because the paracetamol (parrots eat 'em all).

'Doctor, Doctor, I'm suffering from amnesia.'
'Take these pills and you'll soon forget about it.'

'Doctor, Doctor, I've been stung by a bee – shall I put some ointment on it?'
'Don't be silly, it'll be miles away by now.'

'Doctor, Doctor, you know those pills you gave me for my stomach?'
'What about them?'
'They keep rolling off in the middle of the night.'

'Doctor, Doctor, those strength pills you gave me don't work.'
'Why not?'
'I can't get the top off the bottle.'

People living in Elizabethan times rarely took baths. Queen Elizabeth I, who counted herself as cleaner than the average Briton, only took a bath once every three months – 'whether she needed it or not' . . .

King Louis XIV of France never washed . . .

After suffering a skull injury in 1974, Fannie Meyer of Johannesburg, South Africa, drank up to 80 litres of water a day . . .

The average person expels about half a litre of gas each day . . .

'Doctor, Doctor, that ointment you gave me makes my arm smart.'
'You'd better rub some on your head then.'

DOCTOR: Could I have some prepared acetyl-salicylic acid, please?
PHARMACIST: You mean aspirin?
DOCTOR: Oh, yes. I can never remember what it is called.

'Doctor, Doctor, I hate medicine.'
'You don't expect me to swallow that!'

'Doctor, Doctor, are you sure this medicine will cure me?'
'Well, nobody's been back for a second bottle.'

'Doctor, Doctor, my aunt has a sore throat.'
'Give her this bottle of aunti-septic.'

For reasons of camouflage, the sloth never washes and is covered in green moss-like algae . . .

Seventy per cent of household dust consists of shed human skin. The adult human body sheds some 50,000 microscopic flakes of skin every minute . . .

Chaim Soutine, a Russian-born artist, lived in a private suite in the Ritz Hotel in Paris in the 1920s. Soutine never washed or changed his clothes, and when a doctor was asked to examine him because of earache the cause was soon found: a nest of cockroaches was living in the eccentric artist's ear . . .

Isadora Duncan, a famous dancer in the 1920s, was strangled to death when her long scarf became entangled in a rear wheel of the car she was riding in . . .

BOY TO GIRLFRIEND: Darling you look wonderful – what happened?

BOY TO GIRLFRIEND: I'd like to run my fingers through your hair. Can you remember where you left it?

SISTER: Jack is the sweetest, most darling husband in all the world.
BOY: Too bad you married George.

GIRL: If you were my husband I'd give you poison.
BOY: If you were my wife I'd take it.

BOY: May I see you pretty soon?
GIRL: Don't you think I'm pretty now?

GIRL: Where did you get those big eyes?
BOY: They came with the face.

Alexander, King of Greece, was bitten by his pet monkey in 1920 and died from blood poisoning . . .

In one particularly romantic year – 1536 – Henry VIII's first wife, Catherine of Aragon, died; his second, Anne Boleyn, was beheaded, and he married his third, Jane Seymour.

Lucretia Borgia was married four times before she was 22 years old.

Arturo Santora and Barbara Durante had the world's weirdest wedding. They married *on the bottom of the sea* in San Frutosis Bay, with everyone present dressed in deep-sea diving gear. The bride's bouquet was made of coral.

Brigham Young, the American Mormon leader, once married four women in one morning.

GIRL: What has she got that I haven't got?
BOY: Shall I give it to you alphabetically?

BOY: Darling, the whole world revolves around you.
GIRL: Well, I told you not to drink that beer!

What did one raindrop say to the others?
'Two's company, three's a cloud.'

What did the soil say to the rain?
'Go away or my name is mud.'

What did the puddle say to the rain?
'Drop in sometime, I'd be diluted to see you.'

What do skeletons do when they're hit by rain?
Get wet.

Fram Irgard Bruns lived in Berlin in the 1800s. She had six husbands, and they all committed suicide.

Vera Czemsk, a Prague housewife, jumped out of her sixth-floor bedroom window in 1967 after discovering that her husband was planning to leave her. She lived, however, and recovered in hospital – after landing on top of her runaway husband and killing him outright!

Mills & Boon sell 20 million romantic novels each year in Great Britain.

Poet W. H. Auden married the daughter of German novelist Thomas Mann to enable her to obtain a British passport. The first time they met was on their wedding day.

The first pair of false eyelashes was designed in Hollywood.

Queen Elizabeth I was the proud owner of the first wristwatch.

What happened when the wheel was invented?
It caused a revolution.

Who invented the first pen?
The Incas (inkers).

Why was the inventor of the safety match so pleased?
Because it was a striking success.

Who invented the fireplace?
Alfred the Grate.

When was the Iron Age?
Before drip-dry shirts were invented.

Who did not invent the aeroplane?
The Wrong brothers.

How did Benjamin Franklin discover electricity?
It came to him in a flash.

What did Benjamin Franklin say when he discovered electricity?
Nothing. He was too shocked.

DINER: I'll have the soup, followed by the fish.
WAITER: I'd have the fish first if I were you, sir.
DINER: Why's that?
WAITER: The fish is on the turn.

The world's first machine for making holes in doughnuts was patented in 1872 . . .

. . so was the first toothpick machine.

Sweden was the first country to scrap glass milk bottles in favour of paper cartons.

The first bathtub in America was owned by Benjamin Franklin.

The first newspaper headline appeared on the front page of the *New York Gazette* in 1777.

The Wright brothers were the first two men to fly. Unfortunately, Orville Wright was also involved in the world's first fatal aircrash.

Thomas Greene of Maryland ate 350 snails in eight minutes and 29 seconds in 1981 . . .

Donna Maiello of New York ate a hundred metres of spaghetti in 27.75 seconds in 1982 . . .

Dr Ronald Alkana ate 17 bananas in two minutes in 1973 . . .

The world's largest hen's egg was laid in Russia. It contained nine yolks, weighed 400 grams and was 14 centimetres long . . .

There were two provisions shops next door to one another
One put up a sign:
WE SELL OUR BATTERY-PRODUCED EGGS, SOFT
CHEESE AND PATÉ TO THE QUEEN.
The next day the other put up a sign:
GOD SAVE THE QUEEN.

WAITER: We have everything on the menu.
DINER: So I see. Kindly bring me a clean one.

SIGN IN HEALTH FOOD STORE: Closed because of
illness.

'Waiter! There's a fly in my soup!'
'I know, sir, it's the bad meat that attracts them.'

DINER: How often do you change the tablecloths in this
establishment?
WAITER: I don't know, sir, I've only been here six months.

...at Donahue of British Columbia ate 91 pickled onions in ...ne minute and eight seconds in 1978 . . .

...ick Baxter of Derbyshire holds the world record for ...ausage eating: 244 centimetres of sausage in one sit-...ing . . .

Three men claimed a record on 12 April, 1987, after eating 568 winkles out of their shells in 20 minutes at Cromer, Norfolk, to win the Norfolk winkle-picking champion-ships . . .

In 1811, for a bet, a blacksmith at Stroud in Gloucestershire consumed half a litre of winkles, com-plete with shells, in ten minutes. In response to popular demand he then repeated the feat, and died . . .

After losing a bet, Paul Shaw, a farmer from Swindon, Wiltshire, ate 450 grams of fresh grass clippings in 15 minutes on 22 May, 1968 . . .

'Do you know the difference between a hamburger and a old dishcloth?'
'No.'
'Okay, I'll eat the hamburger and you have the dishcloth.'

'Waiter, what's wrong with this fish?'
'Long time, no sea, sir.'

Did you hear the joke about the three eggs?
Two bad.

'Are you sure this ham is cured? It tastes as if it's still sick!'

To commemorate the opening of British Rail's cockney-style pub, the Apples and Pears, at Liverpool Street station in London, John Fletcher of Dover swallowed a hundred whelks in five minutes 17 seconds to claim a world record . . .

To illustrate a lecture on marine biology at St John's College, Minnesota, Professor Daniel Kaiser swallowed 257 live minnows . . .

In 1970 a man called Roger Martinez swallowed 225 live goldfish . . .

Darren Belcher, aged 16, of Cheltenham, Gloucestershire, ate 50 cooked earthworms in 15 minutes on 24 September, 1979 . . .

In a contest in Barnsley, Yorkshire, to see who could eat the most revolting meal, Mick Burton came second with Christmas pudding smothered in gravy, with tripe and sprouts. The winner was Alan Newbold, with six kippers with strawberry jam and jellied eels smeared with lemon curd . . .

A Frenchman called Marc Quinquadon ate 144 snails in 11 minutes 30 seconds in July 1979. On 25 November of the same year, whilst trying to beat his own record, he collapsed and died after eating 72 snails in three minutes . . .

Karen Stevenson of Wallasey, Manchester, speared 2,780 baked beans and ate them one by one in 30 minutes on 4 April, 1981 . . .

Mac Norton, who went under the professional name of the Human Aquarium, once swallowed over thirteen litres of water and 24 live frogs in one go . . .

Which town in Britain makes the unhealthiest sandwiches?
Oldham.

FIRST BOY: I know a café where we can eat dirt cheap.
SECOND BOY: But who wants to eat dirt?

If a crocodile makes shoes, what does a banana make?
Slippers.

WOMAN IN SHOE-SHOP: Can I have a pair of crocodile shoes, please?
SHOP ASSISTANT: Certainly, madam. What size does your crocodile take?

CORONER: And what were your wife's last words, sir?
MAN: They were: 'I don't see how they can make a profit selling this chicken at two pence a pound.'

Karen Stevenson of Merseyside filleted and ate 27 kippers in 60 minutes in 1982 . . .

'Monsieur Mangetout' ate a bicycle in 15 days in 1977. He stewed the tyres and ate the frame as metal filings . . .

Jay Gwaltney of Chicago ate a three-metre birch tree, with a trunk of 12 centimetres diameter, in 89 hours in 1980 . . .

In November 1982, Geoff Derek of Sheffield drank 24 raw eggs from a yard of ale glass in 50 seconds . . .

The Count Dracula Society in California held a dinner in Los Angeles in 1966 at which the guests ate giblet soup, devilled kidneys, baked heart, and sliced liver in brain sauce . . .

The Washington Biological Survey tried to monitor the movements of migratory birds by tagging them with metal labels marked, 'Wash.Biol.Surv.'. A farmer wrote in from Arkansas to complain that he had shot one of the crows and followed the cooking instructions on the leg tag, but the result was far from appetising . . .

In the year 1500BC, the Chinese emperor Ch'eng Tung ordered his chief minister, I Yin, to draw up a list of the most tasty foods in the world. I Yin's catalogue included duckweed from rivers sheltered by yew trees, the tail of the yak, the knees of the elephant, the tails of young swallows and the lips of the orang-utan . . .

There is an annual live minnow eating contest in Geraardsbergen, in Belgium . . .

MAN ON SAFARI: I'd love to swim in that river, but there might be crocodiles in there.
SAFARI GUIDE: No, there aren't any crocodiles.
MAN ON SAFARI: How do you know?
SAFARI GUIDE: Because the piranha fish have chased them all away.

DICK: Would you prefer that a crocodile ate you, or a tiger?
CHRIS: I'd prefer that the crocodile ate the tiger.

What do you get if you cross a maths teacher with a crocodile?
Snappy answers.

Knock knock
Who's there?
Althea
Althea who?
Althea later, alligator.

'Doctor, Doctor, I feel like strawberry blancmange.'
'Sit down, man, and don't be so thick.'

'Doctor, Doctor, this banana diet isn't working on me.'
'Stop scratching and come down from the curtains.'

Why is a camera like a crocodile?
Because they both snap.

n 1978, an elderly African woman was hit on the head by a dog that fell from the sky . . .

The fu-gu fish is a delicacy in Japan. Yet over 200 people die every year from eating it, because the fish is poisonous and needs to be prepared by highly skilled chefs . . .

On 24 August, 1918, near Sunderland, it rained eels for ten minutes. The wriggling creatures covered an area of a quarter of a hectare . . .

A gopher turtle encased in ice dropped in Mississippi in May 1984 . . .

A snowstorm of instant mashed potato fell on King's Lynn in Norfolk in August 1973 . . .

Thousands of thousand-franc notes showered down on Bourges in France in April 1957 . . .

'Doctor, Doctor, I've got bananas growing out of my ears.'
'Good gracious, how did that happen?'
'I don't know, I planted apples.'

A man went to the doctor complaining he was not feeling very well. 'What do you eat?' the doctor asked. 'I eat only snooker balls,' came the reply. 'Snooker balls?' 'Yes, I have yellow and red balls for breakfast, black and brown balls for lunch, and pink and blue balls for dinner.' 'Ah, now I know what your trouble is,' said the doctor. 'You're not eating your greens.'

'Doctor, Doctor, for the last ten years my brother has believed he is a hen.'
'Goodness gracious, why didn't you come to me sooner?'
'We needed the eggs.'

Whooping cough was once treated by putting a live frog in the patient's mouth . . .

For an ordinary cough, the recommended medicine was snails boiled in barley water . . .

Fried mice (fried alive!) were once considered in Britain to be a cure for smallpox . . .

When Prince Henry, eldest son of King James I, caught typhus his physician prescribed a treatment of pigeons pecking at the bottoms of his feet. The prince died, aged 18 . . .

During the American Civil War, maggots were used to clean wounds by eating away the dead tissue . . .

'Doctor, Doctor, my mother thinks I'm crazy because I prefer pink socks to grey ones.'
'What's crazy about that? So do I.'
'Really? How do you like them – fried or boiled?'

'Doctor, Doctor, I feel like a strawberry.'
'So do I – get me one too.'

'Doctor, Doctor, my tongue is as yellow as custard and my legs are as wobbly as jelly.'
'Don't worry – you're just a trifle ill.'

'Doctor, Doctor, I feel like a pink snooker ball.'
'Well get to the back of the queue (cue).'

An adult human contains enough carbon to fill 9,000 pencils; enough water to fill a 45-litre barrel; enough fat to make seven bars of soap; enough salt to fill seven salt cellars; enough phosphorus to make 2,000 matches, and enough iron to make a five centimetre nail . . .

The human kidney contains millions of little tubes. Stretched out in a line, they would extend about 40 miles . . .

If an adult's nerves were stretched out end to end, they would go around the world several times . . .

If an adult's lungs were stretched out, they would cover the area of a tennis court . . .

If you skinned an average adult, the skin would weigh three kilos and cover an area of six square metres.

King Charles II died of a stroke in February, 1685. On the morning the stroke occurred, twelve physicians were charged with the task of 'purging all the poisons' from the king's body. They set to with gusto. After taking two pints of blood from him they shaved his head and singed it with red-hot irons. They then filled his nostrils with sneezing powder and covered his body with hot plasters, which they then ripped off. Amazingly, the king's condition did not improve. So in a last frantic effort the doctors filled him with weird and wonderful potions, including pearls dissolved in ammonia, powdered horse's skull, the skin of frogs and rooks' feathers soaked in ass's milk. Five days later, the king died. The official cause of death was the stroke, but a much more likely killer was the gruesome medical treatment . . .

DOCTOR: I'm afraid you've only got three minutes to live.
PATIENT: Is there nothing you can do for me?
DOCTOR: I could boil you an egg . . .

'Doctor, my family think I'm mad.'
'Why?'
'Because I like sausages.'
'Nonsense, I like sausages too.'
'You do? You must come round and see my collection. I've got hundreds.'

A man called James Morris had skin that was so elastic, he could pull the skin of his chest up over his head. And he could pull his cheeks out more than 20 centimetres from his face . . .

It used to be a common belief that the mucus which runs down your nose when you have a cold was the brain leaking . . .

The human brain weighs about one and a half kilos. Eighty per cent of it is water . . .

Dr Alpheus Meyers of Sheffield, Yorkshire, patented a somewhat drastic cure for tapeworms in 1877. His 'Tapeworm Trap' consisted of a small metal cylinder, tied to a string and baited with food. To make the tapeworm hungry and trappable, the patient ate nothing for several days. The trap was then swallowed, and the tapeworm would poke its head into one end of Meyers' cylinder, where it would be caught by a metal spring. The doctor would then haul up the trap, tapeworm and all. It was a great idea in theory, but after several patients had choked to death it was withdrawn from the market . . .

Before the discovery of anaesthetics, a surgeon's reputation was based on the speed with which he could perform an operation. Baron Dominique Larry, Napoleon's personal surgeon, could amputate a man's leg in just 14 seconds.

One infamous Scottish surgeon, Robert Liston, once amputated a patient's leg in just 42 seconds. Unfortunately for his assistant, he did it so quickly that he also sawed off three of his fingers . . .

'Doctor, Doctor, I keep thinking I'm a strawberry.'
'Hmm. You're really in a jam, aren't you?'

Two men were leaning over the side of a ship, looking rather green. A steward walked up to one of them and said: 'My condolences, sir. Weak stomach, have we?'

'What do you mean, weak stomach?' replied the man, 'I'm chucking it as far as he is!'

The Department of Health lists approximately one thousand different surgical operations that can be performed on the human body . . .

A Norfolk woman complained to her doctor about a pain in her mouth. The doctor got her to say 'Ah', peered inside, and removed a tomato plant that was growing beneath her false teeth . . .

The Swiss insurance company didn't believe the chef who said he had lost a finger in a meat-slicer, so they sent an inspector to investigate. He tried out the machine and lost his finger . . .

Polar bears can outrun reindeer and could probably beat an Olympic swimmer over a long distance swim. Weighing as much as 450 kilos, they can run at speeds of up to 25 miles per hour. They can scent food up to ten miles away, and have been seen swimming at a steady five miles per hour, over a hundred miles from land.

Hair is dead. Hair roots are alive, and they push dead cells up through the scalp. This dead material is what you comb . . .

Your fingernails are made of the same substance as animal claws, beaks, feathers and horns . . .

You can't sneeze with your eyes open . . .

Why was the turkey sitting on an axe?
She was trying to hatchet.

What do you call a bird that steals?
Robin.

What bird is always around when you eat your Christmas dinner?
A swallow.

'I'll tell you what I like about Christmas – kissing the girls under the mistletoe.'
'Really? I prefer kissing them under the nose.'

Why are Christmas trees always warm?
Because they're fir trees.

FIRST CANNIBAL WOMAN: My husband's always moaning about Christmas. I don't know what to make of him.
SECOND CANNIBAL WOMAN: How about a casserole?

The common wood-louse used to be given by medieval doctors to patients suffering from gout or palsy . . .

In the frontier days of America, there were folk remedies for most complaints. People in the northern forests would fasten the right eye of a wolf inside their right sleeve to ward off ill. To rid himself of a birthmark, a frontiersman would rub it with the hand of a corpse or the head of a live eel three mornings in a row . . .

An old tradition says that bread baked on Christmas Eve will never go mouldy.

New Year's Eve is a popular time for predicting fortunes. In Sweden, molten lead is poured into water and the shapes that are formed are used to foretell what the year holds in store.

The image of Santa Claus as a fat old man with white hair and whiskers and dressed in a red suit was the invention of a nineteenth-century artist in America.

Did you hear about the wally turkey?
He was looking forward to Christmas.

How do turkeys communicate?
They use fowl language.

What goes 'gobble, gobble, bang'?
A turkey in a minefield.

Where do all good turkeys go when they die?
To oven.

Knock knock.
Who's there?
Watson.
Watson who?
Watson television on Christmas Eve?

Why did the family of eight cross a turkey with an octopus?
So everyone got a leg for Christmas dinner.

The very first Christmas pudding was a kind of soup with raisins and wine in it.

The leaves on holly trees become less prickly the higher they grow on the tree.

Despite being incorporated into the Christian faith, holly retained many of its pagan associations for hundreds of years after the Druids had ceased to practise their art. Women used to tie it to the ends of their beds to stop themselves from becoming witches.

The turkey was first imported to France by the Jesuits and it is still known in some French dialects as a 'Jesuite'.

Turkeys often look up at the sky during a rainstorm. Unfortunately, many drown as a result.

Believe it or not, there are no turkeys in Turkey.

A group of geese on the ground is called a gaggle. When the gaggle is in the air it becomes a skein.

When it swims a penguin uses its wings as rudders.

Seals can dive to depths of three hundred metres.

The winter of 1592 was so cold that starving wolves entered the city of Vienna and attacked men and livestock.

What do you get if you cross a hush puppy with ice?
A slush puppy.

Why do birds fly south in winter?
Because it's too far to walk.

What do you call a tug-of-war on 24 December?
Christmas Heave.

What did one Christmas cracker say to the other
Christmas cracker?
'I bet my pop's bigger than your pop!'

Which burn longer, the candles on a birthday cake or the
candles on a Christmas cake?
Neither – all candles burn shorter.

Glaciers cover about ten per cent of the earth's surface – almost the same area as the whole South American continent.

Ice is lighter than water.

The river Nile has frozen over only twice – once in the ninth century, and again in the twelfth.

The river Thames froze over in the winter of 1890–91. It was possible to skate the whole length of the river from Lechlade to Teddington.

The winters of 401 and 1642 were so cold in central Asia that the Black Sea froze over.

The winter of 1925 was so cold in Canada that the Niagara Falls were completely frozen.

How do you make anti-freeze?
Send her to the North Pole.

What do you call an alligator at the North Pole?
A cold snap.

What water won't freeze at the North Pole?
Boiling water.

What is the hardest thing about learning to skate?
The ice.

What's the difference between an iceberg and a clothes brush?
One crushes boats and the other brushes coats.

What do angels write on their Christmas cards?
'Halo everybody!'

What do monsters write on their Christmas cards?
'Best vicious of the season.'

What do Christmas bells write on their Christmas cards?
'Let's ring each other in the New Year.'

What does Santa write on his Christmas cards?
ABCDEFGHIJK MNOPQRSTUVWXYZ – (No L, geddit?)

What do sheep write in their Christmas cards?
'Merry Christmas to ewe.'

25 December was not celebrated as the birthday of Christ until AD440.

In 1649, Oliver Cromwell abolished Christmas and declared it to be an ordinary working day. Anybody who celebrated as usual was arrested.

In the nineteenth century, the Post Office used to deliver cards on Christmas morning.

The average iceberg weighs 20 million tonnes.

In 1956 the largest iceberg in the world was discovered in the South Pacific ocean. It was bigger than Belgium.

The amount of water frozen in the Antarctic ice-cap is equivalent to about nine per cent of the Atlantic ocean.

What do cats write on their Christmas cards?
'Wishing you a furry Merry Christmas and a Happy Mew Year.'

What did Adam write on his Christmas card?
'Merry Christmas, Eve.'

What do angry mice send each other at Christmas?
Cross-mouse cards!

BOY: Oh darling, what would it take to make you give me a kiss?
GIRL: An anaesthetic.

BOY: Should a boy kiss with his eyes closed?
GIRL: No, kiss her with your lips.

Did you know that Father Christmas has two addresses, Edinburgh and the North Pole? Letters addressed to TOY-LAND or SNOWLAND go to Edinburgh, but letters addressed to THE NORTH POLE have to be sent there because there really is such a place.

Christmas crackers were invented by Thomas Smith. He had imported some French novelties to sell as Christmas gifts but they did very badly . . . until, that is, he wrapped them up, gave them a snapper, and soon they were going with a bang.

It is not until Twelfth Night (the Feast of the Epiphany) that the figures of the Three Kings are added to the Christmas crib. In Germany, Twelfth Night is known as 'Three Kings Day'.

People from the Philippines have a really strange way of kissing – they put their lips to each other's face and inhale very quickly.

In the film *Don Juan*, starring John Barrymore, there is on average one kiss every 53 seconds.

The first film kiss on Indian screens was not allowed until 1978.

The Chinese did not kiss until the practice was introduced by Westerners. Apparently they're still not very keen on it.

The longest screen kiss ever occurred between Regis Toomey and Jane Wyman in the 1941 film *You're in the Army Now*. Their lip-smacking marathon lasted a breathtaking three minutes!

GIRL: Am I the first girl you've ever kissed?
BOY: Maybe – your face looks familiar.

GIRL: The moment you kissed me I knew it was puppy love.
BOY: Why was that?
GIRL: Your nose was cold.

What do you get if you cross a bee with a bell?
A humdinger.

What bee is good for you?
Vitamin B.

CUSTOMER: Waiter, there's a bee in my soup.
WAITER: Yes sir, it's the fly's day off.

The animal kingdom is not immune from the love bug. Snails kiss before mating – and male Adelie penguins present their chosen partner with a stone, which forms the foundation of their nest. If she accepts, they then stand chest to chest and sing a love song together.

Paul Trevillion and Sadie Nine established the world record for kissing in 1975 – 20,009 in two hours. It is reported that after training, Sadie managed to double the size of her lips.

In cold weather, bees congregate around their honeycombs and shiver. This motion heats up the hive.

A favourite method of execution by the Romans was stinging to death. The condemned person was smothered in honey and exposed to swarms of angry wasps.

Why do bees fly around crossing and uncrossing their back legs?
They're looking for a BP station.

Why do bees have sticky hair?
Because they have honey combs.

'I've just been stung by one of your bees.'
'Show me which one, and I'll punish it.'

'Doctor, Doctor, I think I'm a bee.'
'I'm busy myself – buzz off.'

What is the difference between a sick tiger and a dead bee?
One is a seedy beast, and the other is a bee deceased.

Bees communicate with each other by tail-wagging and whirling. But not all bees speak the same language, because Egyptian and German bees cannot understand each other.

The normal worker bee has to visit nearly 1,500 flowers in order to fill its honey sac. One beehive might store as much as one kilo of honey a day during a good season, a feat that involves about five million individual bee journeys.

Honey bees die immediately after they inflict their sting.

A queen bee only leaves her hive to lead out a swarm and to go away on her wedding night!

Bees were introduced to Australia from Britain.

The only insect to produce food that is eaten by humans is the bee.

Queen bees might lay as many as 3,000 eggs in one day.

The three body segments of an insect do not depend on each other for survival. Some insects can live for as long as a year after their heads have been cut off. They still react to light and heat, even though they can't see where they are going . . .

After mating with the male, the female praying mantis then devours the poor chap whole . . .

Did you hear about the idiot who chased a daddy-long-legs round for two hours until he realised he had a crack in his glasses?

Who is top of the insect charts?
Bug's Fizz.

What goes 99-klonk, 99-klonk, 99-klonk?
A centipede with a wooden leg.

What do you call an Irish flying insect?
Paddy Long-legs.

Ants have five noses . . .

The silkworm moth has 11 brains . . .

A grasshopper's legs can walk on their own, even if they become detached from the creature's body . . .

Whirlwinds, water spouts or even just gusty winds can suck fishes, frogs and goodness knows what else high into the atmosphere, and carry them many miles before releasing them when it rains. Downfalls in this century have included jellyfish in Melbourne, pilchards in Cardiff and frogs in Wigan. But that wasn't all . . .

Flakes of fresh meat fell in Kentucky on 8 March, 1876 . . .

Squashed elderberries rained on Leicestershire in 1950 . . .

Bucket-loads of live winkles fell on St John's in Worcestershire on 28 May, 1881 . . .

In 1804, in Toulouse in France, there was a shower of frogs . . .

A shower of frogs fell on spectators at a military display in Birmingham in 1954 . . .

Millions of seeds from the central African Judas tree fell on the town of Macerata in Italy in 1897 . . .

What do witches sing at Christmas?
'Deck the halls with poison ivy . . .'

TEACHER: Who were the Phoenicians?
PUPIL: The people who invented Phoenician blinds.

What's a biplane?
The last words a pilot says before he bales out.

TEACHER: What did Robert the Bruce do after he watched the spider climbing up and down?
PUPIL: Er, invent the yo-yo?

How did the Chinese discover gunpowder?
It came to them in a flash.

What does Dracula sing at Christmas?
'I'm dreaming of a fright Christmas . . .'

Thousands of live snakes fell on Memphis, Tennessee, on 15 January, 1877 . . .

Tens of thousands of toads fell on Brignoles in France on 23 September, 1973 . . .

Black rain fell on fishermen off the coast of Cornwall in 1959 . . .

Also in 1959, indelible red rain fell on Huddersfield . . .

Hundreds of dead birds fell on the town of Baton Rouge, Louisiana, in 1896 . . .

What do slimmers sing at Christmas?
'A weigh in a manger . . .'

What Christmas carol is popular in the desert?
'O camel ye faithful . . .'

What do elephants sing at Christmas?
'No-elephants, No-elephants . . .'

Knock knock.
Who's there?
Wenceslas.
Wenceslas who?
Wenceslas bus home on Christmas Eve?

What did Noah sing at Christmas?
''Ark the herald angels sing . . .'

What do football fans sing at Christmas?
'Yule never walk alone . . .'

he Royal Family exchange their presents on Christmas
:ve.

.n eccentric French woman, Madame de la Bresse, left a
ortune in her will to provide clothes for snowmen.

The carol 'Silent Night' was written to be accompanied by
a single guitar when the organ in a German church broke
down.

Sir Isaac Newton, Humphrey Bogart and Princess
Alexandra were all born on Christmas Day.

The comedians W. C. Fields and Charlie Chaplin both died
on Christmas Day.

The method for deep-freezing food was invented by an
American called Clarence Birdseye.

Only one in 50 Innuit (Eskimos) has ever seen an igloo, let
alone lived in one.

Knock, knock.
Who's there?
Weevil.
Weevil who?
Weevil work it out.

Did you hear about the idiot caterpillar?
It turned into a frog.

CUSTOMER: Waiter, there's a cockroach in my soup.
WAITER: Yes sir, the fly is on holiday.

'This goldfish you sold me is always asleep.'
'That's not a goldfish, it's a kipper.'

When insects take a trip, how do they travel?
In a buggy.

Which fish go to heaven when they die?
Angel fish.

ost Innuit use refrigerators to stop their food from
eezing.

aper was being made by the paper wasp thousands of
ears before man came up with his 'invention'.

otato crisps were invented by a North American Indian
hief called George Crum.

he American giant water bug paralyses its victim
usually a frog), then sucks all the juices out of its body
o that what is left looks like the original creature –
ut is actually a totally empty shell that collapses the
oment you touch it . . .

he fly's favourite place for laying its eggs is in meat –
referably rotting. Within 48 hours, up to 600 maggots
ave hatched and started to burrow into their surround-
ngs . . .

Twenty-five thousand people a day in America discover
that they have head lice . . .

Parrot fish, inhabitants of undersea coral caves, weave a
blanket of slimy mucus around themselves when they go
to sleep. When they wake in the morning, they shake it off
and swim away . . .

Oysters are ambisexual, which means that they can
change from being a male to a female and back again
several times during their lives . . .

How do goldfish go into business?
They start on a small scale.

'Have you fed the goldfish?'
'Yes – I fed them to the cat.'

What kind of jungle river fish can't swim?
A dead one.

What lies at the bottom of the river and shivers?
A nervous wreck.

Why are goldfish red?
Because the water makes them rusty.

Where do fish wash their fins?
In the river basin.

The most dangerous fish known to man is the electric eel, capable of discharging over 400 volts . . .

The sting of the sea wasp jellyfish causes death within minutes. Found off the coasts of Australia, this nasty creature has claimed 60 victims in the last 25 years . . .

Five piranha fish can eat a horse and its saddle in five minutes flat . . .

The little urchin fish, though less than a foot long, is a deadly shark killer. Its body is covered in spiny points; when it is swallowed by its enemy it can distend itself into a lethal spiky ball. The fish then bores and chews its way out through the shark's stomach, and escapes . . .

TEACHER: Name one animal that lives in Lapland.
PUPIL: A reindeer.
TEACHER: Good. Now name another.
PUPIL: Another reindeer.

What is a Laplander?
A clumsy man on a bus.

How does Jack Frost get to work?
By icicle.

What happens when you slip on the ice?
Your bottom gets thaw.

What sort of sheet cannot be folded?
A sheet of ice.

How do sheep keep warm at the North Pole?
By central bleating.

Why is it difficult to keep a secret at the North Pole?
Because your teeth chatter.

How does Santa dress at the North Pole?
Quickly!

What often falls at the North Pole but never gets hurt?
Snow.

What is white and flies upwards?
A stupid snowflake.

The North Pole is 2,799 metres lower than the South Pole.

No matter how low the temperature falls outside, the windows of an empty house never frost over.

Sound travels so well in the Arctic that on a still day it is possible to hear a conversation from three kilometres away.

It is so cold in Verkhoyansk, Siberia, that boiling water poured from a kettle is solid ice by the time it reaches the ground.

Ten per cent of the salt mined each year is used to de-ice the roads of America.

Ships travel faster in cold water than in warm water.

Knock knock.
Who's there?
Snow.
Snow who?
Snow use asking me, *I* don't know.

What do you get if you cross a shark with a snowman?
Frostbite.

Where do snowmen go dancing?
At the snowball.

What did the snowman say to himself while he was dancing?
'Snow, snow, quick quick, snow . . .'

What is a cold war?
A snowball fight.

On average more snow falls in the state of Virginia, USA, than in the Arctic lowlands.

As much heat is required to melt a kilo of snow at room temperature as is needed to boil a litre of soup.

Clean snow melts slower than dirty snow.

Black snow fell over 18,000 square kilometres of south-east Sweden during Christmas 1969.

There are over 20 words in the Innuit language for 'snow'.

Snow fell on the Sahara Desert in 1979 for the first time in living memory.

What did Sir Walter Raleigh say when he dropped his cloak before Queen Elizabeth I?
'Step on it, kid.'

TEACHER: The ruler of Russia was called the Czar and his wife was called the Czarina. What were his children called?
PUPIL: Czardines?

What did King John wear?
Nothing. He lost everything in the Wash.

What's fruity and burns cakes?
Alfred the Grape.

In February 1887, snowflakes 43 centimetres across fell in Montana, USA.

Snow has fallen on London on Christmas Day only seven times since the beginning of the century.

King Charles II, who ruled from 1660 to 1685, had the rather nasty habit of gathering dust and powder from the mummies of Egyptian kings and rubbing it all over himself – in order to 'acquire ancient greatness'.

The official portrait of the Duke of Monmouth was painted after his decapitation in 1685. This meant stitching the head back on to the body so that it could pose for the artist . . .

Charles VIII of France had six toes on one foot. So worried by this was he that he introduced a fashion for wearing shoes with a square tip so that nobody would notice anything strange about his own foot . . .

Anne Boleyn, Henry VIII's second wife, had an extra finger on her left hand . . .

After the Battle of Waterloo in 1815, the Duke of York had a corridor of his home lined with the teeth of horses which had been killed in battle . . .

King James I put a frog down the Earl of Pembroke's neck – but the Earl got his own back by putting a pig in the king's bedroom.

Why did Henry VIII have so many wives?
Because he liked to chop and change.

TEACHER: In what battle was King Harold killed in 1066?
PUPIL: His last one.

TEACHER: Some English monarchs were Henry VII, Henry VIII, Edward VI and Mary. Who came after Mary?
PUPIL: The little lamb.

'Waiter, waiter, I've had an accident with the salad.'
'What seems to be the trouble, sir?'
'My knife slipped and I cut this slug in half.'

'Doctor, Doctor, I feel like a snail.'
'Mmm, you need to be brought out of your shell.'

Frederick the Great used to have his veins opened in battle to soothe his nerves . . .

To show Queen Elizabeth I how easy it would be to have her rotten teeth removed, the Bishop of London had one of his own teeth pulled out in front of her . . .

King Edward VII often used to hide dead birds in his guests' beds . . .

The Roman snail, the largest snail in Britain, has more than 21,000 teeth . . .

The Kokoa frog of Colombia, South America, secretes a poison so powerful that just 0.1 milligrams is enough to kill a grown man . . .

BOY: I was eating some salad, and I swallowed a slug.
DOCTOR: Goodness! Let me give you something for it.
BOY: No thanks – I'll just let it starve.

'Waiter, I've just found a slug in my salad.'
'Well, that's better than finding half a slug, isn't it?'

What makes a glow-worm glow?
It eats light meals.

TEACHER: Can anyone tell me what sort of insect a slug is?
PUPIL: Yes, sir – a snail with a housing problem.

Where do you find giant snails?
On the end of giants' fingers.

The male Surinam toad smears fertilised eggs over the female's back. The eggs settle into tiny pockets in her outer skin, where they develop. At hatching time, it looks as though hundreds of little toads are bursting out of their mother's back . . .

A San Diego woman was seeking $200,000 damages from a restaurant in California after one of the six snails served to her crawled off her plate . . .

Many lizards, when caught by the tail, let their tails snap off so they can make a fast getaway . . .

If the eye-cup is taken from a frog embryo and cut into small fragments, each fragment will form a smaller, but complete, eye. If the eye-cup is transplanted into the stomach of the frog embryo, then the skin that develops over it will form a lens . . .

Why is the snail one of the strongest creatures?
Because it carries its house on its back.

What is a viper's favourite food?
Hiss fingers.

What's long and green and goes 'hith'?
A snake with a lisp.

What do you do with a green snake?
Wait until it ripens.

What do you get if you cross Dracula with a snail?
The world's slowest vampire.

Did you hear about the stupid woodworm?
It was found in a brick.

Fireflies are bright enough to shine right through the stomach of a frog . . .

Snails can crawl along a razor blade without cutting themselves. This is because they secrete a slimy discharge which enables them to glide over anything . . .

The most poisonous snake in the world is a sea snake which lives off the coast of North West Australia. Careful where you tread when you dash back on to dry land, though: Australia also has the world's most poisonous land snake . . .

Nearly 40,000 people die every year from snake bites. 30,000 of these live (or rather, lived) in India, and most of them are killed by the King Cobra. So deadly is this snake that it can even kill an elephant, by striking at the tip of its trunk . . .

Which hand would you use to grab a poisonous snake?
Your enemy's.

Why did the two boa constrictors get married?
Because they had a crush on each other.

What is a snake's favourite opera?
Wrigoletto.

What do you get if you cross a snake with a government employee?
A civil serpent.

What do you get if you cross an adder with a trumpet?
A snake in the brass.

The African egg-eating snake can stretch its jaws to over four times the circumference of its body in order to swallow its favourite meal. Once guzzled, the egg is broken by the action of the internal spines of the backbone . . .

The world's most poisonous spider is the Brazilian wandering spider. If somebody in Brazil tells you: 'I wouldn't like to be in your shoes', check your clothing carefully . . . because that's where the wandering spider tends to hide itself . . .

The world's largest spider is the African bird-eater. With an extended leg-span of almost 30 centimetres, this hairy monster is just about the size of a dinner plate . . .

What do you get if you cross a glow-worm with a python?
A 20-foot strip-light.

What do you get if you cross a snake with a Lego set?
A boa constructor.

What do you get if you cross a snake with a magic spell?
Addercadabra . . . or Abradacobra.

What happened to the snake with a cold?
She adder viper nose.

What's black and hairy and goes up and down?
A spider in a lift.

Knock knock.
Who's there?
Webster.
Webster who?
Webster Spin, the spider.

CUSTOMER: Waiter, there's a spider in my soup.
WAITER: That'll be 20 pence extra.

What's a spider's favourite television programme?
The Newly-Web Game.

CUSTOMER: Waiter, there's a spider in my soup. Send
me the manager.
WAITER: That's no good, sir, he's frightened of them too.

An unemployed 26-year-old American tried to commit suicide in Massachusetts by thrusting his hand into a cardboard box containing a black widow spider. He lived . . .

Some spiders are used in the manufacture of anaesthetics . . .

Male spiders are often eaten by the female immediately after mating. To ensure their survival, the males of one species offer the ladies a 'present', usually a fly, in the hope that they will have time to mate and get away alive while the gift is still being opened . . .

The greatest recorded number of 'husbands' eaten by a black widow spider is 25 in one day. Perhaps they should have bought her a present . . .

What did Mrs Spider say when Mr Spider broke her new web?
Darn it!

What did the spider say to the beetle?
'Stop bugging me.'

What are spiders' webs good for?
Spiders.

What do baby ghosts like chewing?
Boo-ble gum.

What is the best way for a ghost hunter to keep fit?
Exorcise regularly.

What does a ghost take for a bad cold?
Coffin drops.

In response to a frantic 999 call one night in Basingstoke, Hampshire, Police Sergeant John Barnhard rushed to a lady's house to deal with an intruder. 'He's in the kitchen,' the terrified woman screamed. Charging bravely into the room, Sergeant Barnhard proceeded to tackle the nasty villain who was hiding in the sink – a large, hairy spider which had scared the poor woman out of her wits . . .

The ghost of Borley Rectory in Essex was Marie Lairre, a nun who died in 1667. She appeared 12 times, eventually disclosing at a seance that she was sad because she had not been given a Christian burial. When the rectory was destroyed in 1944, one of the bricks was seen to hover unassisted in the air for a long period of time . . .

The ghost of Polly Nichols has often been seen lying huddled in the gutter in Durward Street, London. Polly was the first victim of the notorious Jack the Ripper . . .

What is a ghost's favourite music?
Haunting melodies.

What do you call twin ghosts who keep ringing doorbells?
Dead ringers.

What game do ghosts like to play at parties?
Haunt and seek.

Who puts the ghosts' point of view at their press conference?
A spooksman.

What do ghosts buy to put in their coffee?
Evaporated milk.

Where do ghosts study?
At ghoul-lege.

Who said 'Shiver me timbers!' on the ghost ship?
The skeleton crew.

What job did the lady ghost have on the jumbo jet?
Air ghostess.

Where do ghouls and phantoms travel?
From ghost to ghost.

Did you hear about the stupid ghost?
He climbed over walls.

Twelve-year-old Anne Hinchfield haunted her home in Ealing for over 50 years after her death. Just before the house was knocked down, a photograph was taken in which appears the ghost-like figure of a young girl . . .

The screams of witches, tortured to death by the Witch Hunter General, can be heard in the dead of night at Seafield Bay in Suffolk . . .

The ghostly footsteps of Mary, Queen of Scots can be heard running down the stairs of Palace House at Beaulieu, Hampshire . . .

At Capesthorne Hall, Cheshire, the ghost of a severed arm gropes around one of the bedrooms at night . . .

What do ghosts put on their roast beef?
Grave-y.

What is the best thing to do if a ghost comes in through your front door?
Run out of the back door.

Did you hear about Romeo Ghost meeting Juliet Ghost?
It was love at first fright.

Why did the skeleton go to the party?
To have a rattling good time.

Nan Tuck's Lane in the village of Buxted, Sussex, is named after a woman who was branded a witch. The villagers tried to drown her in the pond, but Nan escaped and her body was later found hanging in a nearby wood. To this day her ghost has been seen running towards the church, along Nan Tuck's Lane . . .

No fewer than 14 ghosts haunt the Manor House at Sandford Orcas in Dorset, including that of a farmer who hanged himself at the beginning of the eighteenth century. When a family photograph was taken recently on the lawn in front of the manor, the farmer's ghost appeared quite clearly in the group . . .

At Princess Anne's home at Gatcombe Park, Gloucestershire, a huge black headless dog has been seen roaming the lawns . . .

Why did the ghost's shroud fall down?
Because he had no visible means of support.

Why are ghosts always poor?
Because a ghoul and his money are soon parted.

What do you get if you cross the Channel with a sailing ship?
To the other side.

What's 300 metres tall, weighs 7,620 tonnes and attracts bees?
The Eiffel Flower.

What would you get if all the cars in France were red?
A red carnation.

The cave at Loch Katrine in Perthshire is haunted by an evil goblin. Children who go inside it are never seen again . . .

At Bracknell in Berkshire, the ghost of a policeman with a horrifically mutilated face is often seen patrolling the streets at night . . .

The bodies of many plague victims have been discovered at Marnhull in Wiltshire. It is probably the ghosts of two of these that are sometimes seen walking through the darkness, carrying a coffin . . .

Several people have seen the ghost of the Black Nun at the Bank of England. The nun's brother was an employee who was condemned to death for forgery, and it seems she is still searching for him . . .

At Boughton Hall in Surrey, the ghost of an old man smoking a pipe has been sighted on the stairs. The smell of pipe tobacco remains after he has gone . . .

The Channel between England and France gets wider each year by 30 centimetres.

In some parts of Paris there are flush toilets for dogs.

The largest dinosaur egg ever found was discovered in France. It was as big as a rugby ball.

What's a guillotine?
A French chopping centre.

What's one metre tall and rides on the Paris underground?
A Metro-gnome.

What's wrapped in cling film and terrorises Paris?
The lunch-pack of Notre Dame.

What's the best way to keep Britain tidy?
Send all your rubbish to France.

'What's the quickest way to the Gare du Nord station?'
'Run as fast as you can.'

The French eat more cheese per head each year than any other nation.

Nowhere in France is more than 500 kilometres from the sea.

In Pas de Calais, France, there is a river named Aa . . .

There are six million skeletons buried in the catacombs beneath Paris. The chambers were originally quarries used by the Romans over 2,000 years ago.

The most expensive cheese in the world is called La Barratte, and it comes from France.

What's purple and close to France?
Grape Britain.

What do you get if you cross a flat fish with Napoleon Bonaparte?
The flounder of modern France.

HISTORY TEACHER: Can you tell me what happened in 1789?
PUPIL: I can't even remember what happened last night.

GEOGRAPHY TEACHER: Where in France does it never rain?
PUPIL: Under an umbrella.

GEOGRAPHY TEACHER: What is your favourite country?
PUPIL: Czechoslovakia.
GEOGRAPHY TEACHER: Spell it.
PUPIL: On second thoughts I think I prefer France.

GEOGRAPHY TEACHER: How would you describe the rain in the French Alps?
PUPIL: Little drops of water falling from the sky.

FIRST ENGLISH BOY: I'm glad I wasn't born in France.
SECOND ENGLISH BOY: Why's that?
FIRST ENGLISH BOY: I can't speak a word of French.

JACK: Who was the thinnest emperor?
JILL: Napoleon Boneypart

According to a survey carried out at Madame Tussaud's, the most popular person in history was Joan of Arc.

April Fool's Day is known as Fish Day in France.

Steel expands when it is hot, making the Eiffel Tower 15 centimetres taller in summer than in winter.

The French eat about 500 million snails a year.

The word 'biscuit' comes from the French 'bis cuit', which means 'twice cooked'. To preserve them for long periods, the original biscuits had to be cooked twice to make them last longer.

FIRST BOY: Napoleon conquered France, conquered Russia and conquered Italy.
SECOND BOY: Why did he stop?
FIRST BOY: He ran out of conkers.

Where did Napoleon keep his armies?
Up his sleevies.

FIRST GIRL: Your history teacher seems to know the French Revolution inside out.
SECOND GIRL: She should do. She's so old, she was probably there.

Who lost at Waterloo and exploded?
Napoleon Blownapart.

The earliest form of lawn tennis was played by French monks.

Napoleon Bonaparte designed the national flag of Italy.

Napoleon used to travel in a bullet-proof coach.

Napoleon iced cake is named after the emperor, who had a sweet tooth.

Napoleon's wife, Marie Louise, could move her ears at will and even turn them inside out.

Autographs are big business. Emperor Napoleon left 250,000 signatures on various documents, each one worth about £40,000.

BOY: My great-grandfather fought with Napoleon, my grandfather fought with the French and my father fought with the Germans.
GIRL: It seems as if your family couldn't get along with anybody.

BOY: Our teacher was telling us about the Battle of Waterloo today.
MOTHER: What did he say?
BOY: He claimed he was lucky to have escaped with such a minor wound.

TEACHER: Did you know that Columbus found America?
PUPIL: I didn't even know it was lost.

TEACHER: On what date did Columbus cross the Atlantic?
PUPIL: He didn't cross on a date, he crossed on a ship.

What bus sailed the ocean?
Columbus.

TEACHER: Where did Captain Cook stand when he discovered Australia?
PUPIL: On his feet.

Who sailed around Ireland and invented mints?
Marc O'Polo.

What has a mouth, and a fork, yet never eats?
A river.

The most common surname in France is 'Martin'.

Gin was used medically at the Battle of Waterloo. Count Blucher, Field Marshal of the Prussian forces, was thrown from his horse and revived with a rub of the alcohol. He went on to help Wellington defeat Napoleon.

Napoleon Bonaparte suffered from ailurophobia, a fear of cats.

Christopher Columbus only ever signed his name as 'Cristobal Colon'.

Nearly a hundred of the crew that sailed with Columbus to the New World were convicts, specially released for the voyage.

On her second voyage to the New World, the *Mayflower* carried a cargo of slaves.

What do river police use under water?
A squid car.

What does a rower drink at bedtime?
Oar-licks.

What parts of a river can be eaten?
The source (sauce) and the currents (currants).

If you travel due north from Belem, near the mouth of the Amazon, you will not reach land until you arrive at the coast of Greenland.

A hole dug straight through the earth from Shanghai would come out on the other side of the globe near Buenos Aires.

Spain is named after the Carthaginian word meaning 'land of rabbits'.

The British Government offered a reward of £5,000 in 1776 to anyone who could discover the North West Passage.

The British are called 'limeys' because sailors used to eat limes to prevent scurvy.

Eighty per cent of all the species of freshwater fish that live on earth are found in the Amazon.

Cyrus the Great, founder of the Persian Empire, once sentenced a river to death. The river was actually made to disappear for more than a thousand years.

The Canadian river is not in Canada.

A giant waterlily grows in the Amazon which has leaves more than three metres in diameter – strong enough to support the weight of a child.

What's the speed limit in Egypt?
Thirty Niles per hour.

What has four eyes and runs over 2,000 miles?
The Mississippi river. (Four is)

What is denial?
An Egyptian river.

TEACHER: What do you call the small rivers that flow into the river Nile?
PUPIL: Juveniles!

Why should you never swim in the river in Paris?
Because to do so would be in Seine.

What made young Egyptians good children?
They held their mummies in deep respect.

The water drawn up by artesian wells in Australia fell as rain 6,000 years ago.

Enough water flows out of the Amazon each day to supply the USA with 200 times its daily municipal water requirement.

The Egyptians kept dachshunds 4,000 years ago.

The stones from the Great Pyramid at Cheops could be used to build a wall surrounding France at a height of three metres.

The first recorded use of wedding rings was in ancient Egypt, where the circle represented eternity.

Mohammed Ali, an ancient Egyptian ruler, had two infantry regiments consisting solely of one-eyed soldiers.

The ancient Egyptians believed that the earth was hatched from an egg laid by the sacred ibis.

How can you tell when a mummy is angry?
It flips its lid.

What do you get if you cross an ancient Egyptian with a doorbell?
Toot-and-come-in.

What do you get if you cross a vampire with a mummy?
A flying bandage.

Why did the mummy leave his tomb after 4,000 years?
He felt he was old enough to leave home.

What do you get if you cross an Egyptian mummy with a swot?
Someone who is wrapped up in his work.

The 'chadouf', a water raising song, has been sung along the banks of the Nile for 5,000 years.

The original Cinderella was Egyptian.

The famous Egyptian sphinx is a statue of the goddess Armachis. It was carved from a single piece of stone.

Arabic did not become generally spoken in Egypt until the seventeenth century.

Surgeons in ancient Egypt often had their hands cut off if their patients died.

In the Middle Ages nearly one day in three was a religious holiday.

The cheer 'Hip Hip Hooray' is supposed to have originated from the conquest of Jerusalem by the Saracens.

In the Middle Ages the Japanese Imperial army employed special soldiers whose job it was to count the number of severed enemy heads after every battle.

Fish has been served with a slice of lemon since the Middle Ages. The lemon juice was supposed to dissolve swallowed fish bones; only later was it used for taste.

Why did King Arthur have a round table?
So he couldn't get cornered.

What did King Arthur say to the knights of the Round Table?
'Don't just sit there – slay something.'

When were the Middle Ages?
In between the ages that came before and the ages that came after.

Why were the Dark Ages called that?
Because there were lots of knights then.

TEACHER: Castles were surrounded by a moat. Do you know how people crossed the moat to the castle?
PUPIL: In a moatorboat.

What's Camelot known for?
Its good knight life.

What do you get if you cross a comprehensive school with Sir Lancelot?
A knight school.

Why do dragons sleep during the day?
So that they can fight knights.

What does the sea say to the sand?
Not a lot – it mostly waves.

If you wanted to break off your engagement in medieval England you sent your fiancé or fiancée a sprig of lilac.

Women's ears were believed to be highly exciting in the Middle Ages and had to be kept covered.

More English knights were killed by lightning during a thunderstorm in 1360 than were killed at the battles of Crécy and Poitiers.

Admiral Horatio Nelson suffered from severe seasickness throughout most of his life.

The coastline of Canada is six times longer than the coastline of Australia.

What is the difference between a pound and the ocean?
Weight and see.

How much fuel does a pirate ship use?
About 15 miles to the galleon.

Why did the sailor grab a cake of soap when his ship was sinking?
He hoped he would be washed ashore.

What lives in the sea and pulls teeth?
The dental sturgeon.

What is the most untidy part of a ship?
The officers' mess.

Going deeper, the pressure increases in the sea by one atmosphere every ten metres.

A large ship's hull collects a hundred tonnes of barnacles every year.

The Sargasso Sea has no shore. It is entirely surrounded by the Atlantic Ocean.

The total world catch of sea fish represents a little more than five per cent of the amount of edible food produced on land.

The amount of water frozen in the Antarctic ice-cap is equal to roughly nine per cent of the Atlantic Ocean.

What goes into the water pink and comes out blue?
A swimmer on a cold day.

Where is the best place to water ski?
On a sloping area of sea.

What car do dogs like best?
A rover.

What car does Action Man drive?
A Toy-ota.

What car does an electrician drive?
A Voltswagen.

When is a car not a car?
When it turns into a garage.

Only one quarter of all plants grow on land – the rest grow in the oceans.

The water in the world's oceans would fill a pipe 120 kilometres in diameter and stretch nearly one third of the way to the moon.

Every minute, 12 cars are manufactured in the USA.

There are three kilometres of road in Belgium for every square kilometre of land.

A car moving at 88 kilometres an hour will travel more than 17 metres in the time it takes the driver to move his foot from the accelerator pedal to the brake.

The Rolls Royce is classified as a 'compact car' in the USA.

The world's widest road is the Monumental Axis in Brazil – 160 cars could drive side by side along it.

The Jeep got its name from the initials GP, which stood for General Purpose vehicle.

The USSR produces enough oil in one year to power an average car to the sun and back nearly 46,000 times.

In Japan, only the Imperial family is allowed to drive maroon coloured cars.

Why did the man drive his car in reverse?
Because he knew his Highway Code backwards.

What do you call a man with a car on his head?
Jack.

What do you get if you cross a dog with a four wheel drive vehicle?
A Land-Rover.

MAN ON PHONE TO AA: You must help – I've got water in the carburettor.
AA MAN: And where exactly is your car, sir?
MAN: At the bottom of the river.

What did the grape say when the elephant sat on it?
Nothing, it just gave a little whine.

George Thornton was fined for speeding in Cardiff in 1901. He had been driving at ten miles an hour.

On the island of Haiti the local buses are called 'Tap-Taps' because of the noise their diesel engines make.

In ancient Rome, it was customary when toasting a lady's health to drink one glass for every letter of her name.

The correct way to drink Japanese sake is from little bowls or cups that emit a whistling sound when you drink from them.

The Persian poet Firdausi once paid the equivalent of a million pounds for a single glass of beer.

A man called Al Cohol was once arrested in the American city of Seattle. He was charged with drunkenness.

If a drop of whisky is squirted on to its back, a scorpion will sting itself to death.

What happened to the man when a barrel of beer fell on his head?
He came to a bitter end.

What does a dog do that a man steps into?
Pants.

How can you make your tortoise fast?
Don't feed him.

'Why's your dog called Carpenter?'
'Because he does little jobs around the house.'

Did you hear about the wally who insisted on buying a black and white dog?
He thought the licence was cheaper.

Every day for three or four months, every bottle of champagne is gently shaken to make the sediment settle on the end of the cork.

In one North American Indian language, 'Manhattan' means 'the place of drunkenness'.

It takes 40 years for vintage port to reach its ideal state.

A human's body temperature falls when he drinks alcohol.

Teddy bears are named after the American president Theodore Roosevelt, who kept a small bear as a pet.

What did the robot say when it ran out of electricity?
'AC come, AC go.'

What did the mother robot say to the little robot when he came home after midnight?
'Wire you insulate?'

What did the robot say to his girlfriend?
'I love you watts and watts . . .'

What did the wall say to the plug?
'Socket to me, baby.'

What did the electricity meter say to the ten pence piece?
'Glad you dropped in, I was just going out.'

British pets eat 650,000 tonnes of pet food a year, a main ingredient of which is tuna fish. Indiscriminate fishing for tuna leads to the killing of thousands of dolphins every year.

Poodles do not moult.

Cats can draw their claws back into sheaths in their paws.

Dogs wag their tails as a sign of welcome, but cats wag theirs as a sign of warning.

The poet Byron kept a bear as a pet when he was a student at Cambridge.

There is a superstition in certain areas of France that if a bachelor treads on a cat's tail he will not find a wife for at least another year.

Domestic cats spend two thirds of their lives asleep. Their owners spend only one third of their lives asleep.

What's the most shocking city in the world?
Electri-city.

What would you do if you swallowed a lightbulb?
Use a candle instead.

Why did the baker get an electric shock?
He stood on a bun and the currant ran up his leg.

What do you get if you cross William the Conqueror with a power station?
An electricity bill.

Three 25 watt lightbulbs produce less light than one 75 watt bulb.

The average electric eel can produce a shock of 400 volts. Some large eels can generate shocks of 650 volts, enough to kill a man.

The longest stroke of lightning ever measured stretched 32 kilometres across the sky.

The USSR produces enough coal each year to supply London's present electricity needs for over a hundred years.

Direct electric current (DC) cannot be transmitted further than three kilometres.

Shaving with an electric shaver uses less energy than shaving with a hand razor and hot water.

The human brain uses the same amount of power as a ten watt lightbulb.

Another Knight Book

Jeremy Tapscott

THE RAINY DAY SURVIVAL BOOK

This book is here to save you. Packed with 1001 cheap, easy and fun things to do – not just on rainy days but during thunderstorms and even a monsoon! Simply showered with illustrations and positively downpoured with original ideas.

Another Knight Book

Alan Brown

FIRST CLASS

A book of batty beginnings.

Did you know

- that the first teabags were invented by mistake?
- that until the nineteenth century it was illegal to have a bath in Spain?
- that the first lady to wear a swimsuit was arrested for indecent exposure?
- that one of the first cures for toothache was to eat a mouse?

Find out all about these and hundreds more batty beginnings in FIRST CLASS – packed with fascinating and freaky facts to amuse and amaze.

Another Knight Book

Jeremy Tapscott

THE INTER GALACTIC JOKE BOOK

Are you spaced out or simply astronuts? Yes?
Then put on your Apollo-neck jumper and
launch yourself up to planet humour with *The
Inter Galactic Joke Book*.

To boldly joke, where no man has joked
before! Every space joke under the sun, and a
whole lot from even further on. Every one
guaranteed to put you into orbit. You'll be
glad you bought this joke book. In fact, you'll
be over the moon.